MW01252537

ACKNOWLEDGEMENTS

Special thanks to Emma Wright and Rachel Piercey for their kind and meticulous editorial guidance. For notes and other advice, thanks to Richard O'Brien, John Fuller, Avner Offer, Gabriel Rolfe, Douglas Milenko Taylor, Julianne Adams, Marcello Cattaneo, Archie Cornish, and Lorna Oakley.

This book is dedicated to the memory of Lorna Oakley, whose humour and literary judgement were always impeccable.

ABOUT THE POET

Andrew Wynn Owen is an Examination Fellow at All Souls College, Oxford. In 2015, he received an Eric Gregory Award and, in 2014, Oxford University's Newdigate Prize. His first poetry pamphlet, *Raspberries for the Ferry*, was published by the Emma Press in 2014, followed by a collaboration with John Fuller, *AWOL*, in 2015.

ABOUT THE ILLUSTRATOR

Emma Wright studied Classics at Brasenose College, Oxford. She worked in ebook production at Orion Publishing Group before leaving to set up the Emma Press in 2012. In 2015 she was awarded a grant from Arts Council England to run a poetry tour for children. She lives in Birmingham.

OTHER BOOKS FROM THE EMMA PRESS

POETRY ANTHOLOGIES

Slow Things: Poems about Slow Things
The Emma Press Anthology of Age
Mildly Erotic Verse
Urban Myths and Legends
The Emma Press Anthology of the Sea
This Is Not Your Final Form: Poems about Birmingham

POETRY COLLECTIONS FOR CHILDREN

Falling Out of the Sky: Poems about Myths and Monsters
Watcher of the Skies: Poems about Space and Aliens
Moon Juice, by Kate Wakeling
The Noisy Classroom, by Ieva Flamingo (July 2017)

THE EMMA PRESS PICKS

The Flower and the Plough, by Rachel Piercey
The Emmores, by Richard O'Brien
The Held and the Lost, by Kristen Roberts
Captain Love and the Five Joaquins, by John Clegg
Malkin, by Camille Ralphs
DISSOLVE to: L.A., by James Trevelyan
Meat Songs, by Jack Nicholls

POETRY PAMPHLETS

True Tales of the Countryside, by Deborah Alma
AWOL, by John Fuller and Andrew Wynn Owen
Goose Fair Night, by Kathy Pimlott
Mackerel Salad, by Ben Rogers
Trouble, by Alison Winch
Dragonish, by Emma Simon

The Dragon
and The Bomb

An epyllion by Andrew Wynn Owen
Illustrated by Emma Wright

THE EMMA PRESS

THE EMMA PRESS

First published in Great Britain in 2017
by the Emma Press Ltd

ISBN 978-1-910139-58-5

A CIP catalogue record of this book
is available from the British Library.

Printed and bound in Great Britain
by Airdrie Print Services, Glasgow.

theemmapress.com
queries@theemmapress.com

CONTENTS

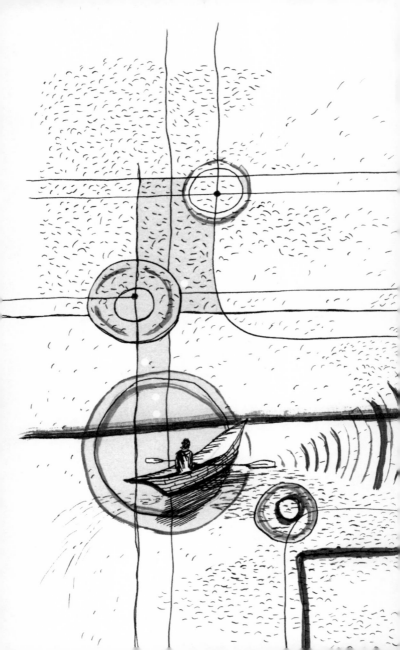

CHAPTER 1.
The Farmer and the Angler

The anchorite, Armando, rose one day
And yawned, 'There's nothing in the sea or sky
To bother me. My life is like a play
Without antagonists – and this is why
I need a change. The saints in time gone-by
Had martyrdoms. But martyrs now? Who cares
For pangs and agonies? The public want affairs.'

So off he sets. He lines a rowing boat
And sculls across the brine. The plish-a-plash
Of oars, disturbing fish, sends out remote
Competing ripples as the crumbled ash
Of breakers blows above the paddle-thrash.
'I live too quietly. I need a feat
To prove at last I'm worthy of the saintly seat.

'The formula is clear: what people like
Is heedlessness that's followed by contrition.
A child, I was an unconforming tyke
But adolescence banished my ambition.
To gallivant is in a great tradition.
It's criminal to leave one's line uncast:
I want a stint of stunts to call "my reckless past".'

With reasoning like this, he hits an island.
He ties his ship and shimmies up a slope
Until he finds a farmstead in the highland,
The sort of spot young lovers might elope.
Beside a weathered copper telescope,
He meets a farmer swigging from a flagon,
Whom Don Armando hails and sues to for a dragon:

'My name is Don Armando and I seek
Adventure, of the dragon-slaying kind.
I'm tired of being labelled "mild" and "meek".
I'd like an epithet that brings to mind
Achilles, Helen – all of Homer's blind
Heroics – and *Orlando Furioso*.
I wish to blaze in life – a hero, not a bozo.

'In short, I yearn for risky escapades
The fame of which will make me feel fulfilled
And win me loving looks and accolades.'
The farmer grunts and checks his flask is filled.
'No dragon here, signor. The last was killed
By Saint Vincenzo, late of Tuscany –
A more impressive saint I know I'll never see!

'For hours he bashed and buffeted the dragon,
The scale-on-skin, the clatter-click of teeth.
With rope he hitched its wagger to his wagon
And dragged it, coughing fire, about the heath
So all the ground was blackened underneath.
I'll never see a scrap like that again.
Today we've neither dragons, nor such daring men.'

Armando slumps, dejected, on a rock,
Running his hands, distractedly, through hair
Besmattered with saltwater and the shock
Of travel. 'By the rood, it isn't fair!'
He pipes, 'I spend eleven years in prayer,
Do all the pilgrimages, live in thrift,
And now, as thanks, th'Almighty cuts me loose, short shrift.'

'Perhaps,' the farmer glugs, 'there is a trick
But, if I tell it, you will have to vow
To do or die. I doubt you'll make a nick
On dragonhide but, if I show you how
To summon it, I'll want you not to bow.
Yes, when it comes to battle, seize your day:
Don't be afraid to bash; don't be abashed to fray.

'Observe,' the farmer sighs, 'the shining city
Below this outcrop. That's the Copper Port.
For years now I've been strapped to write a ditty
About its walls; how, when the sun's half-caught
Behind the eastern hills, its walls are fraught
With swarming dots that chrysalize and dart
Along the swerving valley, toward this island's heart.

'Those houses used to be all weatherboard
And thatch, till one named Haplo Nous arrived
To modernise. He cut the natal cord
Connecting town to mainland, and contrived
Machines so mining on this island thrived.
He ousted every governor in the town,
Of which I was the king. These days, he wears my crown.

'I know that, if I help you, I'll assist
Haplo indirectly, yet I predict
His crafty hand is poised to form a fist
And here he strays. No tinker can conflict
With Ares. Yes, the backlash will inflict
Deserved disaster. He, for all his brains,
Will croak, and I'll descend to dance on his remains.

'To call a drake,' he slowly furls his sleeve,
'You'll need to wield a holy artefact.'
He draws a conch from underneath a weave
Of lapis lazuli. 'A little cracked,'
The king declares, 'but it'll still attract
The dragon – though you'll only have one chance.
Wherever you blow this conch, he'll fly there in a trance.'

With conch and freshened hope, Armando treks
Down the long dune, toward the beach by which
The Copper Port is sprawled. Wing-lifted specks
Disrupt the path of sunbeams, like a glitch
In time, as though some god has flicked a switch
Off and back on – an infinitesimal lapse,
Elided by the slobber of sea, as it slips and slaps.

A swaying angler wades about the shallows
With trousers rolled, a tricorn on her head.
At intervals she bellows, 'To the gallows!'
And 'Trickfins! 'fore I'm done, I'll see you dead.'
She swings her hand in histrionic dread
And spits into the water. Glancing up,
She sees Armando watching and lifts a festive cup.

'Avast to you, landlubber! Do not fret
For me. I know my trade. I am a wader.
This pirate-talk's a get-up to offset
The sameyness of life. I was a trader
At zenith, now I'm just a sand-parader,
And yet I have the sea, and I know this:
Your name's Armando and you're seeking saintly bliss.

'Along your road you'll meet another quester
Who has a destiny all of his own.
His name is Haplo Nous, a famed detester
Of backward thinking: from his makeshift throne
He deems we're still stuck in the age of stone,
And manipulates his instruments to make
Rock sublimate, air vitrify, and water quake.

'Such wilful trifling – well, *de gustibus*.
What comes of him will be his own mistake.
You questers frolic so and never fuss
For what a levy your ambitions take
On others, or what crises you awake.
I, minion of an ancient, should waste no time
With upstart acolytes in search of the sublime.

'But I've a message from my god for you:
The dragon, when it drops, must make a splash.
That's all. Poseidon sent it, so it's true,
And you'll thank me when scale and metal clash.
Like phoenixes, the drake can rise from ash.
Ensure the sea is where you end your quest;
Poseidon, with his warlike seals, will work the rest.'

5

She lifts a lyre of seaweed strung on coral,
And says, 'Before you go, ponder a song
I sing for every mortal. If the moral
Appeals to you, perhaps you'll have a strong
Reason for turning back.' She breathes a long
Abstracted sigh as waves begin to swirl.
'It's called "The Ballad of the Diamond and the Pearl":

'I lost a diamond, found a pearl,
        And threw the pearl away:
I could not bear to wear a gem
        With any hint of grey.

'A pearl is warmer, true, and shines
        But diamonds keep a sheen
Enveloped in their brilliancy
        That time can't contravene.

'I've studied zircon, sapphire, opal,
        Moss agate, malachite,
But none have diamond's millionth-knack
        For congregating light.

'My pearl was bright, my sisters said,
        A dazzling gem to wear,
But diamonds shone inside my dreams
        And nothing could compare.

'A diamond is a latticework
        Of carbon atoms stacked
To disentwine daylight's delight,
        To glisten and diffract.

'It is a shape-retaining stone
    Imprinted on the eye
Long after weaker carbon structures
    Decay and die.

'And yet, in memory, my pearl
    Is warm and soothing still,
Though diamond's cold arrests my heart
    With superfusing chill.

'All roads I used to ramble have
    Receded from my feet,
All stories that I used to love
    Sound incomplete.

'I lost a stone, I found a stone,
    I started from the start
With the only stone I cannot lose,
    My heart.'

With this, the wader paddles through the tide
And, stooping, folds, dissolved below the swell.
Armando gawks as ripples subdivide
And ocean creases, fractures; waves unjell,
Disclosing star, squid, jelly, beasts of shell
That wriggle, writhe, and wrap themselves in knots,
Engorged on spongy plums and hydro-apricots.

A bubbling voice upsurges from the sea:
'Armando, go! Approach the Copper Port
And find the fortified laboratory,
Where Haplo Nous, the alchemist, holds court.
He knows unearthly tricks. He'll help you thwart
The fiery wingster.' Buoyed, Armando turns
And plods toward the port, through dusty dunes and ferns.

CHAPTER 2.
THE LABORATORY OF HAPLO NOUS

The house of Haplo Nous was very odd.
Above the caryatids on its face
Loomed an enormous icon of a god
Twiddling a pair of compasses to trace
Maddening templates round a temple's base.
The doors, as if by magic, opened wide.
Armando steeled himself and shuffled on inside.

Automata were rife in the workshop.
Wheellike contraptions buzzed across the floor,
Exuding acrid scents. A spinning top
Was hurtling down a runway. By the door
A taxidermised lizard, specked with more
Pearls than Armando ever thought existed,
Was curled up like a snake, its carcase fiercely twisted.

High, at the centre of this whirring warehouse,
An elevated, mirror-plated chair
Surveyed a pulpit, like one in a prayerhouse
But weirder, wrought with levers and an air
Of automated function, self-repair,
As though the furniture had grown a mind
To extend the hand and eye by which it was designed.

'It seems you made it,' Haplo Nous remarks
Offhandedly. 'Armando, is it? Sit
On the Komodo lizard. I save the sharks
For pirates. Frantic times. I must admit
I'm staggered that you chose to stick to it,
This rocky road. But smile: you've made the grade
And I'm your friend, my friend, so don't look so afraid.

'I know you met a farmer in the mountains.
That sallow wizard? He detests my work.
The night he left he poisoned wells and fountains
With viper eggs. I toiled to dredge the murk
And make them potable. But I don't shirk
A labour that would kill a lesser mayor.
That's why you'll need my help, Armando Dragonslayer.

'That conch the farmer gave to you is vital.
Its resonance will lure the dragon here.
But I'm the headline. You're a brief subtitle.
You are a puppet, I the puppeteer.
Your dragon, when its downfall comes, shall clear
A path to potencies as-yet-unknown:
The tidal waves it makes will energise my throne.

'You are, *sub specie aeternitatis*, set
To do or die – or do and die – you'll do,
In any case! It hasn't happened yet
And yet it's firm; it's fixed: pre-facto true.
You are among the cherished, chosen few
Who have an earthly task to be completed
And cannot be, before it culminates, defeated.

'This clumpen world is clottish, dot-on-crumb.
I've tried a thousand ways to sift the meld
But stuff is stubborn, knitted, netted, dumb,
And works implacably to pin the weld
Its buckled bits have clustered, woven, held.
I've skinned my fingers fiddling with its weft
But still I cannot say what ballast gives things heft.'

A mania has gripped him. Haplo dashes
Along the shelves, afrenzy, grabbing tomes
That spread their sheaves abruptly, spilling caches
Of multi-coloured parchment. As he roams,
Unflagging robots, anodised with chromes
And pearly silvers, whirr below his feet
To tidy up the mess, then silently retreat.

'Here's Aristotle's *On the Pythagoreans,*
A long-lost work that I, just lately, found.
He claims that what's preserved across the eons
Are facts, pure revelations, which resound
Through human thought and give it solid ground.
He says our nature shows us how we should
Behave – but I have doubts. Can you define the "good"?

'And here's the manuscript of Roger Bacon,
The *Opus Majus*, which he penned to please
His pal, Pope Clement IV: from this, I've taken
The bulk of what adorns this workshop – geez,
There was a maker who could pull a wheeze
And set it soaring.' Haplo splays the book:
'See here. He fashioned barbers' mirrors that could look

'Only at the backs of people's heads
When set in front. He wove a type of rope
From spiders' silk, of which the thinnest threads
Could pull a warship up a sandy slope
Or tether elephants. His lasting hope
Was to invent truth serum for confession.
He failed. Instead, he found a brew to cause digression.

'Alternative realities! They drift
At every corner, floating, sifting, streaming
So colourfully, changeably. The rift
Between their complications and the teeming
Expanse of Now preoccupies my dreaming
And interweaves with waking. The more you look
At life, the more your almost-lives return your look.

'I'd take these doubts down with me to the grave,
Except I love invention – hence machines,
Clamps, levers, cogs, contraptions. I just rave
For innovation: its fizz, its copper greens,
Its shining surfaces, its flawless sheens,
Its intimations of a life to come,
Which tiptaps from its engines like a steelpan drum.'

Haplo smiles, leaps up, and tugs a cord
To reveal a terracotta pot with rods
Of metal sticking out: 'Behold the sword
With which I'll wrest the power of the gods
And re-write history. Not all the squads
And captains of the world could hope to guide
You better for this mission: this dragonicide.

'The principle is simple: caustic soda,
From wood-ash, fizzles on the copper pole.
The ruler of Taipei, in her pagoda,
Had one of these – a "battery" – which she'd roll
Onstage for ceremonies. Once, a foal
Imbibed the liquid and, the legend said,
Before the night was out it grew another head.'

Docile, a pushmi-pullyu toddles by.
A cloud of silent robots tessellate
To form a silver step while more, from high,
Construct a saddle. Haplo, magistrate
Of all their movements, watches them create.
He mounts the steed, enstirruping his shoe:
'As you observe, my friend, the legends were quite true.

'I've made ten thousand of these batteries.
That's why I settled at the Copper Port.
No other town has its capacities
For building projects of the scale and sort
I've set my heart on. Trouble is, I'm short
Of energy: hence you and dragon-slaying.
I've had enough of waiting: it's time for straightawaying.'

He changes tack. 'This ore I've named Uranium,
After the fallen titan of the sky –
It's central to my plan, much like your cranium
Is central to your head. I found it by
Deep mining operations. My supply
Is purified, enriched. When activated,
Perhaps I'll learn, at last, how matter is created.

'The story of survival is the story
Of makers and the miracles they make.
Consider all the talented signori
Who, ages past, gave every breath to break
Our settled limits. Those who overtake
The future make the human spirit strong.
My guiding light's Invention. Hear me sing its song:

'The Golden Age, the Silver Age,
    Both vanished from our view.
Now clanking Copper's all that's left
    But we can make it new.

'We stand, though rarely understand,
    This fragile world of fact,
Deliberating pointlessly
    On where and when to act –

'Not seeing that the only way
    To wriggle from despair
Is a restless, unrelenting quest
    To bring the mind to bear

'On energies, heart-mysteries,
    That make us who we are:
The dragon and the questing saint
    Are children of a star.

'It is our height and, yes, our depth,
        Our strange contamination:
In every human hope, there is
        Destruction and creation.

'The mattock and the willow bark
        Are double-edged, are vague.
The homing pigeon's flap can bring
        Love-letters or the plague.

'Inventions and intentions are
        Ambiguous from birth,
And the salve that rescues humankind
        May mutilate the Earth.

'Could we resolve life's riddle and
        Unpick time's tricky lock,
We'd enter through that doorway where
        The future cannot shock.

'But, every hour, grim Entropy
        Assails our city walls
And will not pause from warfare till
        Invention's tower falls.

'My plan is this: to use the dragon's fall
To push a tidal wave toward the shore,
The force of which will motorise a wall
Of copper rotors hidden at the fore
Of the western beach. Their twist will bring me more
Electric power than burning groves of trees,
And supercharge my stock of buried batteries.

'The surges thus produced will press a piece
Of fundamental matter till it splits.
This moment of division will release
Tinier fragments, spatterings and spits
That topple on like dominoes till it's
Impossible that something won't be smitten.
Lucretius's *De Rerum* will have to be rewritten.

'Perhaps the hills will give forth gilded wheat.
Perhaps it will breathe life in my machines.
Perhaps Lord Zeus will tremble on his seat
And learn, at last, what hesitation means.
Perhaps the island will be smithereens.
Whatever comes, I'll welcome it, resolved
To see the state of human sapience evolved.

'Nor do I fear that feckless farmer-king.
I offered him a place in my new world
But no gift short of palaces would bring
That miser to my side. He'd have me hurled
Out of this island, swept away and swirled
Down maelstroms as a meal for manta rays,
But I've much wilder plans for how to end my days.

'Inventors die when all their work is done
And I've dreamed more designs than might be made
Between today and doom's day. There's no one
Now living on the Earth who can blockade
My progress. Everything has been surveyed,
Predicted and preprogrammed and now you,
My missing piece, arrive. Not too long overdue.

'This is the epoch in which Humour reigns;
    She knocks the crown off Tragedy – and look,
    It was a paper hat! No one complains
    To see old Tragedy deposed. He shook
    Our belfries and our spirits and mistook
    Our crumbling grimace for a crazed encore.
Who'd bother to lament now Tragedy's no more?

    'Yes, now,' the frenzied alchemist exclaims,
    'My years of labour may be justified.
    I have my plans and you the inner flames
    To pummel dragons. And you'll scrap astride
    A gadget that my workshop will provide.
    This is what makes your victory so clinchy:
You'll ride a flight-machine from blueprints by da Vinci.'

    O joy of making, jumble of desire,
    Design of difficulty cut to last.
    Dispersion that we orderers aspire
    To fabricate. A force-field, holding fast.
    Instinctive ghost at which we are aghast!
    You, you alone, can free us from our fix:
Live for us when we're called to mooch across the Styx.

    Live all we launched but could not carry through,
    Live all we hoped the future would become,
    Live all we dreamed (too tentative to do).
    Act, finger-puppet, by our rule of thumb.
    Make of our plans a planetarium,
    And love: love as the seasons love the Earth,
With clarifying death and re-inventive birth.

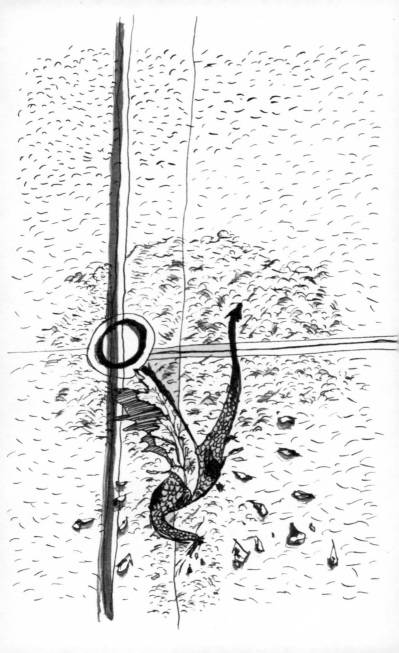

CHAPTER 3.
THE SLAYING OF A DRAGON

The day of tussle dawns. Armando chomps
A bowl of milky oats and downs a skin
Of berry wine. The pushmi-pullyu stomps
And snorts as Haplo's microbots begin
To occupy the air. Green waves sweep in
And out, each one a tenderising force:
Raiders due to erode the coastline in due course.

Wild, Haplo Nous parades his pushmi-pullyu
At pace about the copper battlements.
He tilts his telescope to get a full view
Of all that is unfolding: these events,
So long prepared-for and so long condensed
From cautious fieldwork, now come to fruition
To prove – exactly what? Some murky intuition.

Some vague belief in unseen energy.
Some hunch that if he were to break apart
The building blocks of nature, he might see
Creation as it had been at the start,
Schemata for the whole of time; a heart,
Suspended in the lull between two beats,
From which the secret of the universe secretes.

Armando sets the conch to touch his lips
And huffs a note, which trickles down his arm,
Soaks through his sandals. As a faucet drips,
Vibration dribbles from the conch. Sea's calm
Dissolves as rhythm motorises charm
And tidal waves lurch up to batter sand.
This is a rule of sound: its ripples must expand.

Pure hush. Horizon-watching. Minutes pass
Before – what's that? A red speck in the blue?
Crockery shakes from cupboards. Panes of glass
Vibrate. Then clatter. Then they shatter. Who,
Scared locals ask, could prompt such a to-do?
Steel clock-hands, in the public square, fall still
And star-shaped leaves turn pale, all sapped of chlorophyll.

The speck is magnifying – are those wings?
Clear sky discolours round a roaring weight.
Firm ground is giddy. Nothing stirs or sings
And now it's growing hard to contemplate
Life any other way. Such drakes create
A rupture in the abdomen of time,
These hatchlings of dark matter, gleams of hellish slime.

Its shining mane is sharp as fibreglass,
Its see-through veins are filled with silver oil,
Its eyes are like the eyes of those who pass
Out of our lives before we know them. Coil
On clanksome coil, it buckles up to boil
The acquiescent atmosphere away.
Its motion conjures night out of the natural day.

This beast, it seems of more than three dimensions –
Or should I say, 'More than the usual four'?
Time's a dimension, and I needn't mention
That there are more dimensions – many more!
The fifth, for instance, opens like a drawer
Fitted inside the standard spatial three:
The fifth dimension's built by wishes and ennui.

The sixth dimension is for overloads
And underworlds: there, time squats like a cat
That gurns and grins until its head explodes
And death, shaped like a bristling water-rat,
Swims from the mess. Sometimes, an acrobat
Will slip inside this recondite dimension
By accidental grace, but never by intention.

The dragon saunters now, without a sound,
Across the sky, so high above the sea
He seems more like a comet, from the ground,
Than a lithe and roaring mess of majesty,
Preparing to descend, prepared to free
The particles of everyone below
Out of their fixed arrangements, so blankly neat and slow.

He lands. Quite softly. Did you think he'd stomp?
Ah phooey. He's a dragon, not an oaf.
His landing has a stranger sort of pomp:
He swells and rumples like a rising loaf.
One eye is narrow, one is wide, but both
Blare sharply with – transcending human sense –
A bleak and unbelievable ambivalence.

And yet the instruments of his undoing
Align, unhindered: mirror-plated walls
Designed by Nous to stop this dragon viewing
Its combatant. Soon, as a puzzle falls
Suddenly right, the silver-coated halls
Ingather golden missiles from the sun
And, melting, fusing, blast them at the beast, as one.

Concerted light streaks forth to strike the creature:
He staggers, buckles, screeches, sweeps a claw
To block the glare. His world is bleached of feature.
Yes, where there was so much, there's nothing more
Than scorching pain until, exhausted, sore,
Like light bulbs burst in an electric surge,
The dragon's optic cells swell suddenly and splurge.

The blinded reptile rears his head and roars
So loudly woodlice fall from nearby trees.
He spreads his wings to flap and, launching, soars
Across the bay, above the balconies
Of awestruck onlookers, whose bodies freeze
In terror when the spiky, fuming jaw
Unhinges wide and burps forth magma from his core,

Which drops in caustic goups like molten lead
That melts through ships and walls and metal gates;
It looks like Hell is gushing from his head,
Like Tartarus has burst tectonic plates
And birthed a monstrous god who conjugates
All moods of fire: the superheated blue,
The bronze, the witchwood green, the ultraviolet hue –

Sure, ultraviolet fire, the crazing kind
That only ultraviolent dragons spew!
It doesn't scathe your skin, but sears your mind
Until you can't distinguish what is true
From fiction: dazed, you dribble and eschew
The shelter of your house to roam the streets,
Where lava tucks you, lovingly, below her sheets.

Haplo Nous, high on his pushmi-pullyu,
Now canters round the agora, dodging carts
Of dribbling copper, certain he can pull through
Because he knows his lava-channel charts.
He has his tricks to dodge the dragon's arts:
He waves a hydrophobic gold umbrella
And his fearless pushmi-pullyu's a circumspective fella.

Armando views the mess with sinking heart
But spins and rallies: he knows one more ploy
To thwart this dragon. Drawing forth a cart,
He whips a canvas cover from the toy
That roosts beneath, a jumbled heap of joy:
This is Da Vinci's famous flight-machine
(Quite like a trebuchet combined with a latrine).

The wings begin to flap, the pedals clatter,
The corkscrew mechanism ratchets round,
A hundred spindly levers start to chatter
While everywhere there is a chomping sound
Like moles, in millions, moving underground.
Cramped at the centre, riding wheel and gear,
Don Armando perches and wields a copper spear.

He whizzes this way and the lizard that;
He ducks its tail and dodges underwing.
The spectacle is wild, this mid-air spat
Of dragonhide and lancing copper sting –
A sight disorienting, dizzying,
As canvas vies with leather to assert
Invention's spurring spirit, putting on a spurt.

Meanwhile, the waves are swaying, subdividing
(There's nothing on this earth that's made to stay);
Across the sky see Don Armando gliding
Suave as a senator on the Appian Way
Or pentekonter in Palermo bay.
He spars with all the chutzpah of Wat Tyler;
He darts and dogfights, beagle facing a Rottweiler.

Down on the ground, a grinning Haplo Nous
Is racing through the smog: 'This is my hour!'
He laughs, as lava tips a mountain spruce
On the townhall. A metamorphic shower
Cascades around a falling copper tower,
Dissolving rock and ossifying trees –
A rushing storm of heat, pyrosis with no reprise.

The ocean tantrums at the earth's disruptions
And squids rise up to squelch across the waves;
The tides run in with angular eruptions,
Dispatching fishermen to watery graves,
As sharks take beach-huts for their killing caves.
Paused, Haplo beams to see his new Atlantis
And rubs his palms in glee, much like a praying mantis.

Saltwater rushes through his tidal sluices
And turns the paddled rotors in their ruts.
Poseidon's power is changed to Haplo Nous's
By magnets, springs, coiled wire. Each battery gluts
Its thirst on water's thrust as current cuts,
Then surges in an ecstasy of crackling
And Haplo sets his mind to finish what he's tackling.

Bull's-eye! Armando strikes. The copper slips
Between the scales that plate the dragon's side
And pierces deep. The puncture squeals and drips
A glob of pus – then, ruptured, coughs a tide
Of liquid death. The copper melts inside
As tensile pressure from the dragon's belly
Explodes candescent gore, disgorging blood-flecked jelly.

The flight-machine is streaked with dragonfire
And lurches, limps, erratic in the air.
Its driver now has only one desire:
To aviate home safely, but his hair
Has caught alight. His craft in disrepair,
Before he crashes on a promontory,
Armando sees the dragon, plunging to the sea.

The dragon falls, like Lucifer from heaven.
He conflagrates at nothing, gushing fuel,
Or is it magic? How do dragons leaven
The toxic mixtures that their mouths unspool?
The heat they lose must leak by kilojoule.
This yowling dragon falls like Lucifer
And, thrashing, lies transfixed on a trident's middle spur.

The water shakes, adjacent waves unlatch,
And from the froth? Poseidon surfs, to shout,
'A dragon? Well, I never – what a catch!
Let's make it more marine.' His fingers spout
A spray of salt: sharp, gleaming dorsals sprout
Along the spine, the lizard's sandy tinge
Turns oily, and the scales take on a silver fringe.

Through all this morphic fun, let's not forget
That dragons, quite like us, are sentient.
A drake's not social, nor a household pet,
But each is born with undefined intent
And would live well, if only we'd relent:
This dragon had been born detested, hunted,
So there's no wonder that his moral sense was blunted.

Not far, back in his workshop, Haplo Nous
Has split an atom's nucleus. The fission
Reaction fizzes. Now there is no use
For doubts or double-takes as, in partition,
Uranium begins the chain emission
Of neutrons, three by three, an exponential
Growth pattern that unleashes the force of its potential.

Fizzcrack! Kaboom! Derailment, death, and doom
Go chomping through the city. Nothing stands.
Dumbfoundingly and inchingly, a plume
Of radiated sediment expands
In mushroom-cloud above the island sands.
Uranium's cell-torturing perfume
Rips through the region like the rush of the Simoom.

The blast unfurls, obliterating all
Within a radius of twenty miles.
Nihility disperses nature. Tall
And terrible, a storm of shadow piles
Across the sea in wind-directed aisles.
Now fire and water fuse as plasma-fire
To mangle the remains of Haplo's copper wire.

But Haplo isn't finished. Not by far.
Precisely at the second he succeeded,
Old Saturn, long-retired Olympian Tsar,
Decided, with a lurch, that Nous was needed:
Up from the ground, eruptive hellhounds speeded
To drag his body through a swirling portal
Of fire. And that's how Haplo Nous became immortal.

And Haplo Nous's last invention? Gone.
Obliterated by its own success.
Yet rumour spreads. 'All lost?' 'Was it a con?'
And alchemists, in unison, confess,
'Compared to this, our tinkering was dress.'
Olympus quakes with sudden overhauls:
As Haplo Nous ascends, his predecessor falls.

Ares, called 'mainomenos', 'alloprosallos'
(Or 'raving one' and 'this-way-that' for his trick
Of siding with no side), has lost his palace
From which, all callousness, he used to flick
The dominoes of death. His rhetoric
And proschemata dissipate like mist
Till, on the throne of war – a world-upturning twist –

See Haplo Nous, the maker of The Bomb,
Enforce his hell with nothing but a threat.
The gods look round, amazed. 'Where is he from
And where did Ares go? For all his sweat
And mess, I liked him.' Through her steel lorgnette,
Queen Hera glares: 'Who dares unseat my son?'
But Haplo stares her down. His rise can't be undone.

Since Haplo did what Haplo knew he would,
The world has altered. In the atomic age,
It doesn't do to go misunderstood
And history falls open at a page
Where governments, so cautious, must engage
New diplomats, who speak in bleaker style,
Promising peace – as Brecht says, for some and for a while.

These days, confusing peace with terror, we
Imagine constant trembling for our lives
The best solution to brutality.
Yet still, submerged in all of us, survives
Some precious wish for liberty, which thrives
Most fiercely when it lacks the light. It's clear
The Bomb must be destroyed, if we're to conquer fear.

Yes, who can now believe The Bomb is good?
Who still believes in weapons of that type?
Some did because they theorised it would
Reveal utopias they hoped were ripe
For harvest. But such wonderlands are hype.
You might blame Heisenberg or Harry Truman,
But we are all complicit. All of us are human.

No, this is not the kindly sort of story
In which the innocent make getaways
(For them, there'll be no sequel). In a gory
Vicissitude of tide, the dragon strays
(Now newly squidified) into a maze
Of seaweed where a roaming band of sharks
Ambush the muddled creature and bite till teeth spit sparks.

Meanwhile, Armando was beatified
And later canonized for dragon-slaying.
I wouldn't like to slate what's ratified
By papal bull, or go about nay-saying
And poking holes – but I can't help dismaying
To see the crimes that hide in golden paint:
How can one be a killer and a holy saint?

All will be ash, and wind will bear that ash
Across, between, above, beyond, around
Our silent cities. 'Our'? No, surely rash
To claim dominion of any ground?
We own ourselves. We own, perhaps, the sound
Expulsed and fashioned by our lungs and tongue.
Ice age? Inferno? Comet? Let the sling be slung.

Enough of all downbeatery! I said
I'd pen a piece concerned with dragon-slaying
And look, I did – though, true, I lost the thread
Of narrative a while back. What I'm saying
(And fear I'm scarcely coping at conveying)
Is simply this: we should respect the dragon
And stop our stories short, before they start to drag on.

THE EMMA PRESS
small press, big dreams

The Emma Press is an independent publisher dedicated to producing beautiful, thought-provoking books. It was founded in 2012 by Emma Wright in Winnersh, UK, and is now based in Birmingham. Having been shortlisted in both 2014 and 2015, the Emma Press won the Michael Marks Award for Poetry Pamphlet Publishers in 2016.

The Emma Press is passionate about making poetry welcoming and accessible. In 2015 they received a grant from Arts Council England to travel around the country with *Myths and Monsters*, a tour of poetry readings and workshops for children. They are often on the lookout for new writing and run regular calls for submissions to their themed poetry anthologies and poetry pamphlet series.

Sign up to the monthly Emma Press newsletter to hear about their events, publications and upcoming calls for submissions. Their books are available to buy from the online shop, as well as in bookshops.

https://theemmapress.com
http://emmavalleypress.blogspot.co.uk